BOUNCING BACK

A WORKBOOK ON RESILIENCE

STACY ZEIGER
BUILDING KIDS' CHARACTER
Seattle, WA

Resilience (*n.*) – the ability to adapt and recover from adversity or moments of change that come up in life.

Synonyms: flexibility, elasticity, endurance

Related words: strength, courage, fortitude, stamina, backbone

Contents

What Is Resilience? 3

    Resilience in Nature 5

    Why It's Important to Be Resilient 7

Who Are You? 8

Strengths and Weaknesses 12

Setting Goals 14

    Effective Goal Setting 15

    Setting Short-Term Goals 16

    Thinking About Your Goals 17

    Setting Long-Term Goals 20

    Reaching Your Goals 22

Other Ways to Be Resilient 23

Developing Rituals and Routines 24

    Prioritizing Tasks 27

Juggling Emotions and Responsibilities 31

    Celebrity Spotlight: J.K. Rowling 32

    The Power of Optimism 33

    Expressing Yourself 37

    Expressing Yourself Positively 38

    Creating a Support Network 43

Setting Boundaries 46

Conflict Resolution 48

    Conflict-Resolution Strategies 49

Developing Character Traits 50

    Caring 50

    Equality 52

Summing It Up 54

Resources to Learn About Resilience 55

GLOSSARY 58

What Is Resilience?

Have you ever faced something that is really hard? It may be something small, like breaking a bone, feeling left out or losing a game. It may be something bigger, such as dealing with your parents' divorce, losing someone close to you or regularly being bullied or harassed.

Resilience is the ability to bounce back from these types of situations. Instead of letting something get you down, you use it to build you up and become a stronger, more focused person. Instead of being sad and quitting, you keep going.

Resilience in Your Life

Stop and think about your own life. Have you faced any major changes? Any situations that have caused you a lot of stress and sadness? Take a moment and write down some of the challenges that you've had to face or that you're currently facing.

Now look at that list of challenges and think about how you've handled or are currently handling them. Are you sad and angry? Do you think things will never get better? Or are you trying to make things better? Do you know that, in the end, everything will be okay?

> *"When I'm stuck with a day that's gray and lonely, I just stick out my chin and grin and say the sun'll come out tomorrow."*
>
> - "Tomorrow"

Have you ever seen the movie *Annie?* Maybe you've just heard the song. How can looking on the bright side and remembering that "the sun'll come out tomorrow" help you be resilient?

> *"I have missed more than 9,000 shots in my career. I have lost almost 300 games. On 26 occasions I have been entrusted to take the game-winning shot... and I missed. I have failed over and over and over again in my life. And that's precisely why I succeed."*
>
> - Michael Jordan

Think about what you already know about resilience. How does the quote above show Michael Jordan's resilience?

> "What doesn't kill you only makes you stronger."

Maybe you have heard this quote before. Do you think it's true? How can bad things make you stronger?

Resilience in Nature

> *"The strongest oak of the forest is not the one that is protected from the storm and hidden from the sun. It's the one that stands in the open where it is compelled to struggle for its existence against the winds and rains and the scorching sun."*
>
> - Napoleon Hill

One of the best places to learn about resilience is in nature. While some human activities have an effect on the resilience of nature, nature is generally fairly resilient when it comes to facing adversity.

Think of the small trees sprouting from the ground after a forest is destroyed in a fire.

Think of trees that fall but continue to grow new branches and leaves in different positions.

Think about the flowers that grow in the cracks of the sidewalk, the weeds that you're constantly pulling up from the garden but that always reappear and the dandelions that may cover your yard in the summer.

> *"The bamboo that bends is stronger than the oak that resists."*
>
> - Japanese Proverb

Think about the Japanese proverb and the pictures of nature. What can nature teach you about being resilient or bouncing back in the face of adversity?

Why It's Important to Be Resilient

Sometimes it's hard to be resilient. You may feel like your life is over or that there is no way out of your troubles. You may be embarrassed or feel like no one will understand your problems and emotions. When you're at the bottom (or feel like you are), you have two choices: stay at the bottom or get back up.

> *"Inside of a ring or out, ain't nothing wrong with going down. It's staying down that's wrong."*
>
> - Muhammad Ali

Chances are you've seen at least one sports movie in your life. You know the type – the football player looks like he'll never make it into a game, the horse breaks a leg and will never race again, the boxer is knocked down and rises at the last second. Imagine how different movies like *Rudy, Seabiscuit, Cinderella Man, Rocky, Miracle, We Are Marshall* and *Pride* would be if the main characters were not resilient.

Think About It

A boxer is in the ring. He has reached the 12th round of a title fight. His opponent knocks him down. The referee starts counting to ten. The boxer is in some pain, but he could easily get back up. He has a choice to make: stay down and end the round or get back up and potentially win the fight. Answer the questions in the boxes below, being sure to consider the future consequences of the boxer's decision (future fights, career, what people think of him, etc.).

What happens if the boxer stays down?	What happens if the boxer gets back up?

Who Are You?

In order to be resilient, you have to know who you are. How do you describe yourself? Are you the kid who isn't very smart, the girl who barely speaks English, the boy without a father, the kid without a home, the girl who isn't very pretty or the boy who is different and bullied on a daily basis? While negative things are a part of your life, they do not have to be who you are. Neither do the opinions of others.

> "No one can make you feel inferior without your consent."
>
> - Eleanor Roosevelt

Being resilient requires knowing who you are and having a positive opinion of yourself. Words that describe a resilient person include: strong, tough, unsinkable, determined, optimistic, responsible.

Do these words describe you? If not, what changes can you make so they describe you better?

1. I am (can be) strong when....

2. I am (can be) tough when...

3. I am (can be) unsinkable because...

4. I am (can be) determined to...

5. I am (can be) optimistic about...

6. I am (can be) responsible for...

Now it's time to get to know yourself a little more.

Describe yourself in writing or by drawing a picture.

Let's think about your positive traits a little more...

1. What are three positive adjectives that describe you?

2. A special committee has decided to honor you for something great. What award will you receive?

3. How would the people who are closest to you and like you best describe you?

If you had trouble answering these questions, you should take some time to discover the positives inside of you. Some ways to do this include:

1. Challenge yourself to look in the mirror and spend a minute telling yourself how great you are.
2. Make a list of the things that you like about yourself.
3. Ask the people close to you what they like about you.
4. Find a few pictures of yourself and tape positive adjectives to them. Glue them in a notebook or hang them on your mirror or beside your bed.

The Town Mouse and the Country Mouse

from Aesop's Fables

One day a country mouse in his poor home
Received an ancient friend, a mouse from Rome:
The host, though close and careful, to a guest
Could open still, so now he did his best.

He spares not oats or vetches: in his chaps
Raisins he brings and nibbled bacon-scraps,
Hoping by varied dainties to entice
His town-bred guest, so delicate and nice,
Who condescended graciously to touch
Thing after thing, but never would take much,
While he, the owner of the mansion, sate
On threshed-out straw, and spelt and darnels ate.

At length the townsman cries: "I wonder how
You can live here, friend, on this hill's rough brow:
Take my advice, and leave these ups and downs,
This hill and dale, for humankind and towns.
Come now, go home with me: remember, all
Who live on earth are mortal, great and small:
Then take, good sir, your pleasure while you may;
With life so short, 'twere wrong to lose a day."

This reasoning made the rustic's head turn round;
Forth from his hole he issues with a bound,
And they two make together for their mark,
In hopes to reach the city during dark.

The midnight sky was bending over all,
When they set foot within a stately hall,
Where couches of wrought ivory had been spread
With gorgeous coverlets of Tyrian red,
And viands piled up high in baskets lay,
The relics of a feast of yesterday.

The townsman does the honours, lays his guest
At ease upon a couch with crimson dressed,
Then nimbly moves in character of host,
And offers in succession boiled and roast;
Nay, like a well-trained slave, each wish prevents,
And tastes before the tit-bits he presents.

The guest, rejoicing in his altered fare,
Assumes in turn a genial diner's air,
When hark! a sudden banging of the door:
Each from his couch is tumbled on the floor:
Half dead, they scurry round the room, poor things,
While the whole house with barking mastiffs rings.

Then says the rustic: "It may do for you,
This life, but I don't like it; so adieu:
Give me my hole, secure from all alarms,
I'll prove that tares and vetches still have charms.

1. What was the problem with the country mouse?

2. What lesson did the country mouse learn?

3. Did the country mouse end up being happy with what he had and who he was?

Strengths and Weaknesses

Knowing your strengths and weaknesses can help you develop resilience. When you know what you're good at, you can use it to your advantage. When you know where you are weak, you can build up that area or avoid it.

Think about yourself.

What are you good at??

What are you bad at?

> "Build up your weaknesses until they become your strong points."
>
> - Knute Rockne

How can you turn what you are bad at into what you are good at?

You have the potential to accomplish anything you want to.

What are some things you want to accomplish in your life?

> "Shoot for the moon. Even if you miss,
> you'll land among the stars."

What does this quote mean?

How can this quote help you?

Setting Goals

Setting goals can help you overcome whatever life throws at you. Having goals gives you a sense of purpose and something to take your mind off the struggles you may face. To get anywhere, you have to know where you want to end up.

Take a look at the stories of these two students:

Kara wanted a new bike. Her mom told her she would never be able to get a new bike because they just did not have the money. Kara got mad at her mom and moped in her room. She was jealous of her friends who had bikes and was mean to them. Because of this, she lost a lot of her friends. Instead of figuring out a way to get a bike or trying to enjoy life without one, she decided to be miserable.

Alicia wanted a new bike too, but her parents also did not have the money. Alicia decided that even though they did not have the money, she would do whatever it took to get a new bike. Summer was six months away, and Alicia was going to have a new bike by summertime. Since it was Christmas, Alicia made Christmas cards and sold them to her neighbors. She asked some of her aunts and uncles if she could help them out around the house for a little money. She sold a few of the toys she did not play with anymore. By the time summer came, Alicia had enough money to buy a new bike. It was not the coolest bike, but it was a bike! And she had bought it all by herself.

1. What attitude did Kara have?

2. What attitude did Alicia have?

3. How did having a goal help Alicia?

4. What could Kara learn from Alicia?

Effective Goal Setting

In order for goal-setting to be successful, you have to ask yourself the following questions:

1. What is my goal?
2. Is it possible to reach my goal?
3. How am I going to reach my goal?
4. How long will it take me to reach my goal?
5.
6. Who can help me reach my goal?

When you set goals, you want to make short-term and long-term goals. A short-term goal is something you can do in a few days or a few months. A long-term goal is something it will take you much longer to do, like a year or more. Good goal-setters set both kinds of goals. Reaching your short-term goals helps you reach your long-term goals.

Why do you think that is?

Always put a time limit on your goals. For example, Alicia wanted to have a bike by summer. A time limit makes you work harder to reach your goals.

Why do you think a time limit makes you work harder?

Some examples of good goals are:

1. Save $100 in a year.
2. Pass my current grade.
3. Not get a detention for a week.
4. Help my mom out by loading the dishwasher for a month.
5. Get all my homework done by 7 p.m. each night.

Setting Short-Term Goals

Short-term goals are designed to be completed quickly. You may set a goal to complete in a few weeks or a few months. No short-term goal should last longer than six months.

What are some examples of short-term goals?

- o If you have just come to the United States, your goal may be to find someone at school to help you learn English.
- o If you have recently lost a parent, your goal may be to talk to your school counselor and find a support group.
- o If you are homeless, your goal may be to find a place to live.
- o If you have a disability, your goal may be to learn something that is a challenge for you.

What are some short-term goals you can set?

1.

2.

3.

4.

5.

Thinking About Your Goals

Remember these questions about goals?

1. What is my goal?
2. Is it possible to reach my goal?
3. How am I going to reach my goal?
4. How long will it take me to reach my goal?
5.
6. Who can help me reach my goal?

For every short-term goal you wrote down, you should answer these questions.

GOAL #1

1. What is my goal?

2. Is it possible to reach my goal?

3. How am I going to reach my goal?

4. How long will it take me to reach my goal?

5. Who can help me reach my goal?

GOAL #2

1. What is my goal?

2. Is it possible to reach my goal?

3. How am I going to reach my goal?

4. How long will it take me to reach my goal?

5. Who can help me reach my goal?

GOAL #3

1. What is my goal?

2. Is it possible to reach my goal?

3. How am I going to reach my goal?

4. How long will it take me to reach my goal?

5. Who can help me reach my goal?

GOAL #4

1. What is my goal?

2. Is it possible to reach my goal?

3. How am I going to reach my goal?

4. How long will it take me to reach my goal?

5. Who can help me reach my goal?

GOAL #5

1. What is my goal?

2. Is it possible to reach my goal?

3. How am I going to reach my goal?

4. How long will it take me to reach my goal?

5. Who can help me reach my goal?

Setting Long-Term Goals

A long-term goal is any goal that will take you six months or longer to complete. Sometimes you have to set long-term goals for things that may happen way in the future and will take a lot of effort to reach. Maybe you want to graduate from high school. Maybe you want to be an astronaut. Maybe you want to get a new place to live, buy something expensive or be nicer to your sister and brother. Maybe you want to learn to read better. These are all long-term goals.

My long-term goals are…

1.

2.

3.

You have to make a plan to reach your long-term goals, but it can be a lot harder than with short-term goals. Reaching a long-term goal takes a lot of steps.

For example, if you want to learn to read better, what kinds of things do you think you will have to do?

To learn to read better, you will have to learn the alphabet, practice reading, find someone to read with, read a lot of different books at different levels, practice spelling words, maybe see a reading tutor and take some reading tests. You may not read better at first, either. It will take time.

Choose one of your long-term goals and write a plan for reaching that goal. If it's hard to write what you want to do, you can also draw pictures.

My goal is _____.

To reach my goal, I am going to:

Remember the questions to ask when you set goals too:

1. What is my goal?
2. Is it possible to reach my goal?
3. How am I going to reach my goal?
4. How long will it take me to reach my goal?
5.
6. Who can help me reach my goal?

Reaching Your Goals

You've just taken a big step toward reaching your goals by writing them down. Studies have shown that people who write down their goals are more likely to reach those goals than people who do not. Other steps that help people reach their goals are:

- Set realistic goals (you already did that too!).
- Use a mix of short-term and long-term goals (you're 3 for 3!).
- Tell someone else about your goals.
- Visualize reaching your goals.

Do you have someone you can share your goals with? It could be a friend, a family member, a social worker, a counselor, a pastor. Look for someone who has your best interest in mind. It does not have to be someone you are extremely close with, just someone you know will help keep you on the right track.

I am going to share my goals with:

1.

2.

3,

The final step toward reaching your goals is visualizing yourself reaching them. How do you do that? Here are a few ways:

- Take your goal and turn it into an "I am" phrase and repeat it to yourself every day. For example, "I am a high school graduate" or "I am a great English speaker."

- Go to a quiet place, close your eyes and think of yourself after you have reached your goals. If your goal is to graduate high school, you may visualize your graduation ceremony. If your goal is to learn English, you may visualize yourself having a conversation with a stranger.

- Draw a picture of yourself after you meet your goal.

- Make a large poster of your goals and put it where you will see it every morning.

- Write down all the good things that will come from meeting your goals.

Take a moment and use one of these strategies to visualize meeting your goal.

What strategy did you use?   How did it make you feel?

Other Ways to Be Resilient

By having something to look forward to, you have less time to let the hardships of life bring you down, but setting goals is just one of many ways to help you learn how to develop resilience. The more of these strategies and attitudes you develop, the easier it will be to become a resilient person.

Some of the ways to be resilient include:

- Developing rituals and routines
- Prioritizing tasks
- Juggling emotions and responsibilities
- Being optimistic
- Gaining control of a situation
- Learning to express yourself
- Handling stress properly
- Finding people to confide in
- Staying healthy
- Setting boundaries
- Using conflict-resolution strategies

Can you add anything to the list? What healthy strategies have you used to overcome challenges and difficult life situations in the past?

> "Adversity is a fact of life. It can't be controlled. What we can control is how we react to it."
>
> - Unknown

Developing Rituals and Routines

Rituals and routines are actions or sets of actions we do on a regular basis. You may follow a certain routine when you get up in the morning. Your family may have certain rituals they follow during the holidays, such as always serving the same meal or setting up the Christmas tree on a specific day.

What are some of your rituals and routines?

How can having rituals and routines help you develop resilience and overcome adversity? By giving you some stability. No matter what problems you are facing, chances are there's a lack of stability. If you're homeless, you may not know where you'll sleep tonight. If you've recently lost a parent, life is a lot different than it used to be.

When you follow rituals and routines, you bring things into your life that you can depend on when times get rough. If those rituals and routines are interrupted, you can create new ones to help you cope with the adversity you face. When life is full of change, you need something you can count on.

If you do not have rituals and routines, think of the things in your life that remain the same. These constants can help you get through the hard times.

Take one of your rituals, routines or constants and write a short poem about it.

Pittypat and Tippytoe

by Eugene Fields

All day long they come and go---
Pittypat and Tippytoe;
Footprints up and down the hall,
Playthings scattered on the floor,
Finger-marks along the wall,
Tell-tale smudges on the door---
By these presents you shall know
Pittypat and Tippytoe.

How they riot at their play!
And a dozen times a day
In they troop, demanding bread---
Only buttered bread will do,
And the butter must be spread
Inches thick with sugar too!
And I never can say "No,
Pittypat and Tippytoe!"

Sometimes there are griefs to soothe,
Sometimes ruffled brows to smooth;
For (I much regret to say)
Tippytoe and Pittypat
Sometimes interrupt their play
With an internecine spat;
Fie, for shame! to quarrel so---
Pittypat and Tippytoe!

Oh the thousand worrying things
Every day recurrent brings!
Hands to scrub and hair to brush,
Search for playthings gone amiss,
Many a wee complaint to hush,
Many a little bump to kiss;
Life seems one vain, fleeting show
To Pittypat and Tippytoe!

And when day is at an end,
There are little duds to mend;
Little frocks are strangely torn,
Little shoes great holes reveal,
Little hose, but one day worn,
Rudely yawn at toe and heel!

Who but *you* could work such woe,
Pittypat and Tippytoe?

But when comes this thought to me:
"Some there are that childless be,"
Stealing to their little beds,
With a love I cannot speak,
Tenderly I stroke their heads---
Fondly kiss each velvet cheek.
God help those who do not know
A Pittypat or Tippytoe!

On the floor and down the hall,
Rudely smutched upon the wall,
There are proofs in every kind
Of the havoc they have wrought,
And upon my heart you 'd find
Just such trade-marks, if you sought;
Oh, how glad I am 't is so,
Pittypat and Tippytoe!

1. What does the speaker like about Pittypat and Tippytoe?

2. How does this ritual/routine/normal event make the speaker feel?

3. What are a pittypat and tippytoe?

Prioritizing Tasks

Part of developing rituals and routines and setting goals is determining what tasks and what people are most important on a daily basis. What's most important to you? Doing well in school? Spending time with friends? Learning to play an instrument? Participating in a club, a band or a special hobby? Exercising and staying healthy?

List the ten things you do every week that are most important to you or mean the most to you.

1.

2.

3.

4.

5.

6.

7.

8.

9.

10.

Now list the ten things you spend the most time on every week.

1.

2.

3.

4.

5.

6.

7.

8.

9.

10.

Do your two lists match up? You may have a few things on the second list that you cannot really change, such as eating, getting dressed or going to school. But do you also have activities on the second list that you wish weren't there or that you wish you spent less time on?

Look at Yolanda's two lists:

The Ten Things I Do Every Week that Are Most Important to Me

1. Eating dinner with my family
2. Playing volleyball
3. Student council sessions
4. Shopping with my mom
5. Hanging out with my friends
6. Watching my favorite show on TV
7. Playing games with my sister
8. Doing my homework
9. Talking to my parents
10. Going running

The Ten Things I Spend the Most Time On

1. Getting ready for school
2. Arguing with my sister
3. Sleeping
4. Moping in my room
5. Watching TV
6. Going running
7. Listening to music
8. Using Facebook
9. Texting friends
10. Playing volleyball

1. Do the things that are most important to Yolanda match up with the things she spends the most time on?

2. What are some changes Yolanda could make to her priorities?

Like Yolanda, Jared found that his list of what was most important didn't match up with the things he spent the most time on. Take a look at Jared's lists:

The Things that Are Most Important to Me

1. Spending time with my family
2. Spending time with my friends
3. Going to school
4. Playing baseball
5. Going to church
6. Exercising and staying healthy
7. Looking my best
8. Relaxing and watching TV
9. Spending time online
10. Writing

The Things I Spend the Most Time On

1. Hanging out in my room
2. Avoiding my parents
3. Trying to talk to my friends
4. Staying home from school and playing video games
5. Sitting on the bench at baseball games
6. Sleeping
7. Writing in my journal
8. Reading Facebook messages and comments
9. Looking my best
10. Pretending to be sick

You may notice that Jared does not do most of the things that are important to him. Many of the things he does are negative. Jared is bullied a lot at school. Kids who used to be his friends make fun of him. His parents do not pay a lot of attention to him.

What can Jared do to overcome his situation?

Take another look at your own lists.

1. If there are things that are important to you that you do not spend a lot of time on, what can you change to make more time for those things?

2. Are there any negative behaviors or activities on your second list? If so, what causes them? What can you do to get rid of them?

When you refocus your priorities and spend time on what's important to you, it is easier to be resilient. This may mean cutting back the time you spend with friends who are bad influences to spend more time with your family. If you receive negative messages online, you may want to cut back your computer use and focus on talking to people who make you feel good about yourself. If you spend time doing drugs or feeling depressed, ask someone you trust for help. Doing something for someone else or taking up a new hobby may help you feel better too.

Juggling Emotions and Responsibilities

Sometimes your negative emotions can keep you from dealing with your responsibilities. Other times, they can spur you to action. As you learn to be resilient and overcome adversity, you have to learn to handle your negative emotions positively so they do not keep you from fulfilling your responsibilities.

Take a look at these two stories:

Jason's mom had a list of chores he and his brother had to do after school. Jason always got mad because his brother never did his chores and Jason would get blamed for it. Instead of doing his chores, Jason decided he just wasn't going to do anything either. He came home from school every day, sat on the couch and watched TV. Jason's mom was upset. She had to work two jobs to help the family make ends meet and needed Jason and his brother to help out around the house. Instead of spending time with her boys when she came home, she had to spend time doing chores because Jason and his brother were not willing to help out.

Amaya moved to the United States from South Africa. She did not speak English very well, and kids made fun of her. Amaya had a hard time because her parents did not speak English very well either. She was embarrassed and scared to be in a new country, but instead of letting it get the best of her, she asked her teacher for help. Her teacher helped Amaya learn English. She made a few friends. She felt better about herself and was able to help her parents too.

The two stories above show both ends of the spectrum.

1. How did Jason's decision to handle his emotions negatively hurt his family?

2. How did Amaya's decision to handle her emotions positively help her family?

3. How have you handled your emotions when you've had a difficult situation with your family?

31

Celebrity Spotlight: J.K. Rowling

You probably know J.K. Rowling as the author of the *Harry Potter* series, but it's likely you do not know the struggles she went through before finding success.

Before publishing the *Harry Potter* series, Rowling was a single mother contemplating suicide. Without a job and with a failed marriage, Rowling felt like she would never make anything of herself. Instead of letting depression and a lack of money take over, Rowling poured her emotions and energy into finishing *Harry Potter*. Once the book was finished, she submitted it to 12 publishers, and all of them rejected it. Thirteen proved to be Rowling's lucky number. On the 13th try, her book was finally accepted by a publisher and became the thing that would turn her into a billionaire.

In June 2008, Rowling was asked to give the commencement address at Harvard University. Her speech to the graduates included the following bits of wisdom to help you as you work toward developing resilience:

"Ultimately, we all have to decide for ourselves what constitutes failure, but the world is quite eager to give you a set of criteria if you let it."

"Failure gave me an inner security that I had never attained by passing examinations. Failure taught me things about myself that I could have learned no other way. I discovered that I had a strong will and more discipline than I had suspected; I also found out that I had friends whose value was truly above the price of rubies."

"Life is difficult, and complicated, and beyond anyone's total control, and the humility to know that will enable you to survive its vicissitudes."

"We do not need magic to change the world. We carry all the power we need inside ourselves already: we have the power to imagine better."

The Power of Optimism

Studies have been done to show the power of optimism in overcoming adversity and illness. Multiple studies have shown that optimistic thinking has been a key factor in cancer survival rates. Even cancer patients with a terminal form of the illness who were optimistic lived significantly longer than those who just gave up.

Being optimistic doesn't mean you're never going to have negative thoughts, feel upset or get depressed. It means you don't let the negatives take over. That's hard work sometimes, especially when it seems like you're being hit with one negative after another or are stuck in a situation that feels like it will never end.

Try some of these strategies to overcome the negativity and develop an attitude of optimism:

1. Choose to wake up on the right side of the bed every morning.
2. Spend less time with negative people and choose to be nice instead of saying negative things about people.
3. Take care of yourself by eating well, getting enough sleep and exercising.
4. Keep a collection of motivational quotes or sayings.
5. Take time to participate in positive activities you enjoy.
6. Do something nice for someone else.
7. Seek out humor: watch a funny movie, read some jokes, act silly.
8. Listen to upbeat music.
9. Be flexible.
10. Focus on your successes and learn from your failures.

Which of these strategies do you think could help you most?

Why is being optimistic so powerful?

The Emperor's New Clothes

by Hans Christian Andersen

Once there was an Emperor who loved new clothes. He loved new clothes so much that he spent all his money on them. The Emperor had so many new clothes that he had a different suit for each hour of the day. Rather than spending time making decrees and consulting with officials, this Emperor spent his time in his dressing room, changing his clothes.

Still, everything went well in the Emperor's town and it enjoyed a wealth of visitors. One day, two special visitors entered the town. They called themselves weavers and said they knew how to weave clothes with beautiful colors and elaborate patterns. In fact, their clothes were so exquisite that they could only be seen by those who were worthy of seeing them. Plain folk, poor folk, and those who didn't understand fine fashion would never notice how great their clothes were.

These men greatly impressed the Emperor. He thought he could use such a set of clothes to help weed out some of the foolish people who worked for him. The Emperor ordered the weavers to make him a suit immediately.

The two weavers pretended to set up shop. Then they sat at their looms and pretended to work very hard. However, the two men were not really working, but just pretending to work. They asked the Emperor's staff to provide them with silk and gold thread, but instead of weaving them on the looms, they put them in their own bags and continued to pretend to work.

After some time, the Emperor wanted to see their progress. He remembered that only the wise and deserving would see the clothes and was a bit worried that he himself wouldn't be able to see the suit the weavers were making. So instead of going to see the suit himself, he sent his wisest, most sensible worker to view the suit.

When the Emperor's worker entered the hall where the weavers were working, he thought something must surely be wrong. "I cannot see anything on the looms," the worker thought in his head, but he said nothing aloud.

The weavers talked with the worker and asked him what he thought about the suit they were making. So the worker looked again and still saw nothing. He realized that if he said he could not see anything, they would think he was not wise or fit to view the suit so he replied, "This is an excellent suit! I will tell the Emperor how beautiful it is and how much I love the pattern and the colors."

"Thank you," said the imposters. They described the pattern and the colors to the worker so he would be sure to give the Emperor the proper details about the suit that was being made.

The Emperor was pleased by his worker's report, but he wanted to get someone else's opinion, so he decided to send his wise, old secretary to check on the weavers. When the secretary arrived at the hall where the weavers were working, he thought something must surely be wrong.

The weavers saw the confused look on the secretary's face and said, "Whatever is the matter? Do you not find our work as beautiful as the other worker the Emperor sent?"

The secretary didn't want the weavers to think he was stupid, so he told them that the suit was indeed beautiful. The weavers then described the pattern and colors so the secretary could share the information with the Emperor.

After both men gave favorable reports to the Emperor, the whole city started talking about how great the suit was going to be. The Emperor decided he wished to see it himself. He went to the hall where the weavers were working.

"Isn't it beautiful?" said the two men whom the Emperor had sent ahead of him. They pointed at the empty looms and described the colors and patterns the weavers had told them they contained.

"What is going on?" thought the Emperor. "There's nothing on those looms. This is terrible. Am I really not fit to see their clothes?" However, out loud, the Emperor said "Why, the suit is charming. It's beautiful! Magnificent! I love the colors and the pattern!"

Everyone around him said the same, although none of them could actually see anything on the loom.

The Emperor decided he would wear his suit during a procession the next day. The weavers pretended to work all night to prepare the suit for the Emperor. They rolled the cloth off the looms. They cut the air with scissors. They sewed needles without any thread. In the morning they proclaimed, "The Emperor's new clothes are ready!"

As the two weavers pretended to dress the Emperor they told him the clothes were as light as a cobweb. They described the pants, the jacket, and the scarf. The Emperor still couldn't see anything, but he didn't want to appear unfit for the clothes, so he kept his mouth closed.

The Emperor headed outside to board his float for the royal procession. All of the people in the city lined the streets waiting to see the Emperor's clothes. As the float moved through the street, the people were shocked to see the Emperor wearing nothing, but not wanting to appear unwise or stupid, they cried out, "Oh how beautiful are your new clothes! They fit so well and the color is exquisite!"

The Emperor was so pleased by the reaction. None of his suits had ever been this impressive. The people continued to heap on the praise until the float passed a young child.

"The Emperor has nothing on," the child laughed.

Soon the other people in the city started whispering what the child said and finally started crying out "The Emperor has nothing on!"

Laughter roared through the streets and suddenly the Emperor realized he had been tricked. Still he continued on with the procession, a bright smile on his face, as if he was wearing the most beautiful suit in the world.

1. What was important to the Emperor?

2. Did the Emperor have a good group of people around him?

3. Why did the child tell the truth?

4. How did the Emperor show resilience when he realized he had no clothes on?

Expressing Yourself

Being optimistic and developing resilience isn't about holding your emotions in. In fact, when you hide your emotions and refuse to tell people how you really feel, it can be harder to be positive and endure difficult situations. Learning to express your emotions in healthy ways can make situations easier to handle and can help you gain control over those emotions.

Negative Ways to Handle Your Emotions

Do you handle your emotions in any of the following negative ways?

- Becoming withdrawn and depressed
- Turning to food or something else for comfort
- Getting angry and yelling/screaming
- Becoming violent
- Throwing things
- Throwing up
- Self-harm

If you have handled your emotions negatively, how did that make you feel?

Instead of the negative actions above, try expressing your emotions in the following positive ways:

- Talking it out with someone
- Writing a letter
- Channeling your emotions into a positive activity
- Meditating or using another relaxation strategy
- Keeping your cool
- Finding something to laugh about

Expressing Yourself Positively

Put yourself in the shoes of these kids. Read each scenario and explain how you would positively handle the emotions you'd feel in these situations.

1. Zoe was recently expelled from school for getting into a fight with another girl. She's mad at the girl for picking the fight and mad at the principal for not giving her another chance.

2. Jorge was recently diagnosed with cancer. His friends are afraid to be around him, and his doctor told him he can't play soccer anymore. He's bored, lonely and scared.

3. Cat's mom just kicked her dad out of the house. Cat's mad at her dad for ruining their family, mad at her mom for not doing more to keep her dad around and sad that her family is falling apart.

4. Ram just moved to the United States. In school, kids tease him because of his accent and ask if he's a terrorist because of how he looks. He's becoming embarrassed of his family and his heritage.

5. Max has been in and out of foster homes his entire life. He just wants someone to love him and pay attention to him, so he acts out by stealing and vandalizing public property.

A Little Princess

by Frances Hodgson Burnett

Chapter One: Sara

Once on a dark winter's day, when the yellow fog hung so thick and heavy in the streets of London that the lamps were lighted and the shop windows blazed with gas as they do at night, an odd-looking little girl sat in a cab with her father and was driven rather slowly through the big thoroughfares.

She sat with her feet tucked under her, and leaned against her father, who held her in his arm, as she stared out of the window at the passing people with a queer old-fashioned thoughtfulness in her big eyes.

She was such a little girl that one did not expect to see such a look on her small face. It would have been an old look for a child of twelve, and Sara Crewe was only seven. The fact was, however, that she was always dreaming and thinking odd things and could not herself remember any time when she had not been thinking things about grown-up people and the world they belonged to. She felt as if she had lived a long, long time.

At this moment she was remembering the voyage she had just made from Bombay with her father, Captain Crewe. She was thinking of the big ship, of the Lascars passing silently to and fro on it, of the children playing about on the hot deck, and of some young officers' wives who used to try to make her talk to them and laugh at the things she said.

Principally, she was thinking of what a queer thing it was that at one time one was in India in the blazing sun, and then in the middle of the ocean, and then driving in a strange vehicle through strange streets where the day was as dark as the night. She found this so puzzling that she moved closer to her father.

"Papa," she said in a low, mysterious little voice which was almost a whisper, "papa."

"What is it, darling?" Captain Crewe answered, holding her closer and looking down into her face. "What is Sara thinking of?"

"Is this the place?" Sara whispered, cuddling still closer to him. "Is it, papa?"

"Yes, little Sara, it is. We have reached it at last." And though she was only seven years old, she knew that he felt sad when he said it.

It seemed to her many years since he had begun to prepare her mind for "the place," as she always called it. Her mother had died when she was born, so she had never known or missed her. Her young, handsome, rich, petting father seemed to be the only relation she had in the world. They had always played together and been fond of each other. She only knew he was rich because she had heard people say so when they thought she was not listening, and she had also heard them say that when she grew up she would be rich, too. She did not know all that being rich meant. She had always lived in a beautiful bungalow, and had been used to seeing many servants who made salaams to her and called her "Missee Sahib," and gave her her own way in everything. She had had toys and pets and an ayah who worshipped her, and she had gradually learned that people who were rich had these things. That, however, was all she knew about it.

During her short life only one thing had troubled her, and that thing was "the place" she was to be taken to some day. The climate of India was very bad for children, and as soon as possible they were sent away from it—generally to England and to school. She had seen other children go away, and had heard their fathers and mothers talk about the letters they received from them. She had known that she would be obliged to go also, and though sometimes her father's stories of the voyage and the new country had attracted her, she had been troubled by the thought that he could not stay with her.

"Couldn't you go to that place with me, papa?" she had asked when she was five years old. "Couldn't you go to school, too? I would help you with your lessons."

"But you will not have to stay for a very long time, little Sara," he had always said. "You will go to a nice house where there will be a lot of little girls, and you will play together, and I will send you plenty of books, and you will grow so fast that it will seem scarcely a year before you are big enough and clever enough to come back and take care of papa."

She had liked to think of that. To keep the house for her father; to ride with him, and sit at the head of his table when he had dinner parties; to talk to him and read his books—that would be what she would like most in the world, and if one must go away to "the place" in England to attain it, she must make up her mind to go. She did not care very much for other little girls, but if she had plenty of books she could console herself. She liked books more than anything else, and was, in fact, always inventing stories of beautiful things and telling them to herself. Sometimes she had told them to her father, and he had liked them as much as she did.

"Well, papa," she said softly, "if we are here I suppose we must be resigned."

He laughed at her old-fashioned speech and kissed her. He was really not at all resigned himself, though he knew he must keep that a secret. His quaint little Sara had been a great companion to him, and he felt he should be a lonely fellow when, on his return to India, he went into his bungalow knowing he need not expect to see the small figure in its white frock come forward to meet him. So he held her very closely in his arms as the cab rolled into the big, dull square in which stood the house which was their destination.

It was a big, dull, brick house, exactly like all the others in its row, but that on the front door there shone a brass plate on which was engraved in black letters:

MISS MINCHIN,
Select Seminary for Young Ladies.

"Here we are, Sara," said Captain Crewe, making his voice sound as cheerful as possible. Then he lifted her out of the cab and they mounted the steps and rang the bell. Sara often thought afterward that the house was somehow exactly like Miss Minchin. It was respectable and well furnished, but everything in it was ugly; and the very armchairs seemed to have hard bones in them. In the hall everything was hard and polished—even the red cheeks of the moon face on the tall clock in the corner had a severe varnished look. The drawing room into which they were ushered was covered by a carpet with a square pattern upon it, the chairs were square, and a heavy marble timepiece stood upon the heavy marble mantel.

As she sat down in one of the stiff mahogany chairs, Sara cast one of her quick looks about her.

"I don't like it, papa," she said. "But then I dare say soldiers—even brave ones—don't really LIKE going into battle."

Captain Crewe laughed outright at this. He was young and full of fun, and he never tired of hearing Sara's queer speeches.

"Oh, little Sara," he said. "What shall I do when I have no one to say solemn things to me? No one else is as solemn as you are."

"But why do solemn things make you laugh so?" inquired Sara.

"Because you are such fun when you say them," he answered, laughing still more. And then suddenly he swept her into his arms and kissed her very hard, stopping laughing all at once and looking almost as if tears had come into his eyes.

1. How did Sara and Captain Crewe handle troubles?

2. How did Sara and Captain Crewe express themselves positively?

3. What can you learn about troubles from Sara and Captain Crewe?

Creating a Support Network

In order to talk out your emotions and feel secure, you need to build a support network. Your support network should be made up of positive influences and people you can go to when you're feeling sad, depressed, overwhelmed or angry. The people in your support network should all have your best interest in mind.

Who can be in your support network?

- Friends
- Parents
- Other family members
- Teachers
- Counselors
- Pastors
- Church members

You need to trust the members of your support network enough to share what you're feeling. They cannot help you if you're not honest with them.

Right now, think of at least ten people who could be a part of your support network. If you have trouble thinking of ten people you know well, it's okay to include people who do not know you very well but are still a positive influence in your life, such as teachers or the school counselor.

1.

2.

3.

4.

5.

6.

7.

8.

9.

10.

If you can think of more than ten, that's okay too. The more people in your network, the more people you will have to go to when you face problems.

The Constant that I Need

By Stacy Zeiger

"I'll always be there for you," she said.
And it's true, she always was.
Always the first to wipe my tears
And the first with her applause.
I never really understood
Why she was always there.
When other things mattered more
She's the one who always cared.

Of course it wasn't always good.
I didn't like her on my case.
I told her just to back away
And get out of my face.
I didn't need her there for me.
I could do it on my own.
She went away and I soon found
That I was all alone.

Only when I was all alone
Did I realize what I'd lost.
It wasn't like I thought it'd be.
I didn't like the cost.
And so I went crawling back to her
Tears streaming from my eyes.
I told her I was sorry
And she just looked at me and sighed.

"I'll always be there for you," she said.
And it's true, she always was.
Always the first to wipe my tears
And the first with her applause.
Even when I forget
Just how much she means
She's always waiting for my return.
The constant that I need.

1. What lesson did the speaker of this poem learn?

2. Why was the person the speaker mentions in the poem important?

3. Do you have anyone in your life who resembles the person the speaker references in the poem?

The Lion and the Mouse

from Aesop's Fables

Once, as a lion lay sleeping in his den, a naughty little mouse ran up his tail, and onto his back and up his mane and danced and jumped on his head so that the lion woke up.
The lion grabbed the mouse and, holding him in his large claws, roared in anger. 'How dare you wake me up! Don't you know that I am King of the Beasts? Anyone who disturbs my rest deserves to die! I shall kill you and eat you!'

The terrified mouse, shaking and trembling, begged the lion to let him go. 'Please don't eat me Your Majesty! I did not mean to wake you, it was a mistake. I was only playing. Please let me go - and I promise I will be your friend forever. Who knows but one day I could save your life?'

The lion looked at the tiny mouse and laughed. 'You save my life? What an absurd idea!' he said scornfully. 'But you have made me laugh, and put me into a good mood again, so I shall let you go.' And the lion opened his claws and let the mouse go free.

'Oh thank you, your majesty,' squeaked the mouse, and scurried away as fast as he could.

A few days later the lion was caught in a hunter's snare. Struggle as he might, he couldn't break free and became even more entangled in the net of ropes. He let out a roar of anger that shook the forest. Every animal heard it, including the tiny mouse.

'My friend the lion is in trouble,' cried the mouse. He ran as fast as he could in the direction of the lion's roar, and soon found the lion trapped in the hunter's snare. 'Hold still, Your Majesty,' squeaked the mouse. 'I'll have you out of there in a jiffy!' And without further delay, the mouse began nibbling through the ropes with his sharp little teeth. Very soon the lion was free.

'I did not believe that you could be of use to me, little mouse, but today you saved my life,' said the lion humbly.

'It was my turn to help you, Sire,' answered the mouse.

Even the weak and small may be of help to those much mightier than themselves.

1. What does the story of the Lion and the Mouse show about caring about others?

2. How did the mouse end up helping the lion?

3. How does this story show the importance of having different types of people around to help you?

Setting Boundaries

> "Boundaries are to protect life – not limit pleasures."
>
> -   Edwin Louis Cole

Setting boundaries for yourself can help you develop resilience and keep you from encountering situations that trigger negative attitudes, emotions or behaviors. Your boundaries may include avoiding certain people or places, talking with someone in your support network before making key decisions.

Determine the boundaries that you need to set by answering these questions:

1. What activities have a negative effect, cause negative emotions or turn you into someone you don't like?

2. What people have a negative influence on you?

3. What places bring out the worst in you or tempt you to behave in negative ways?

4. What times of the day, the week, the month or the year are the toughest for you?

5. What triggers negative emotions in you?

Use these answers to determine your boundaries. When writing your boundaries, begin with phrases such as "I will…," "I will not…" or "Others will not…" Examples of boundaries include "I will not associate with people who smoke or drink" or "Others will not raise their voices with me."

Come up with three boundaries to start with:

1.

2.

3.

Sticking to your boundaries is hard work. You have to learn how to tell people "no," tell people when they have crossed a line and walk away from situations that come close to crossing the boundaries you have set for yourself. If your boundaries include cutting out people who have a negative influence on you, you can expect other people to make fun of you or try to make you feel guilty about it.

Share your boundaries with the members of your support network. They will be the people who back you up and praise you for sticking to your boundaries. They will also remind you of your boundaries when you're in danger of crossing them.

Do not be discouraged if you find yourself crossing your boundaries at first. When you're not used to having boundaries, it can be difficult to follow them. Gradually, you will learn to stick to your boundaries. As you do, you may discover other people, places and situations that trigger negative emotions and behaviors. Add to your boundaries and revise them as necessary. As you develop resilience, you may find that you no longer need your initial boundaries.

Conflict Resolution

Learning healthy ways to resolve conflict can help you stick to your boundaries and become more resilient.

What do you do when something makes you angry or when someone does something you don't like?

Responses to conflict typically fall in one of three areas:

- Passive
- Aggressive
- Assertive

Passive Response to Conflict

When you respond to conflict passively, you don't deal with it. Instead, you ignore the conflict, hide how you may be feeling or react nonverbally.

Aggressive Response to Conflict

When you respond to conflict aggressively, you deal with the conflict negatively and may not resolve anything. You yell. You call people names. You hit. You throw things or slam doors. You make threats.

Assertive Response to Conflict

When you respond to conflict assertively, you work to resolve the conflict. You listen to all sides of the story and apologize if you were at fault. You express how the conflict made you feel and act politely while talking it out.

Conflict-Resolution Strategies

If you find yourself using passive or aggressive strategies for dealing with conflict in your life, try some of these strategies to deal with conflict more positively.

Resolving Conflict with Others

1. Bring in a third party to help you deal with the conflict. Use a counselor, a teacher or a peer mediator. You want someone who will listen to the facts before giving an opinion.

2. Use "I" statements to acknowledge your feelings. Say something like, "When X happened, I felt…"

3. Take time to chill out before dealing with the conflict.

4. Focus on the problem, not what's wrong with you or anyone else involved.

Resolving Conflict with Yourself

1. Forget the past and focus on living in the present and moving forward.

2. Don't worry about what other people think.

3. Listen to your intuition.

4. Use "I" statements with yourself to identify how certain conflicts make you feel.

5. Think about making your life and your world better.

Think about a current conflict in your life that you have put off dealing with or a past conflict that you handled poorly. How could you use these strategies to deal with that conflict?

Developing Character Traits

When you're faced with a crisis, adversity and other situations that require resilience, certain character traits can help you face that adversity and develop resilience.

Caring

> "Caring about others, running the risk of feeling, and leaving an impact on people, brings happiness."
>
> - Harold Kushner

Do you agree with the quote from Harold Kushner?

When you step outside of yourself and your problems to show care for others, you take the focus off your problems and refocus your energy into helping others. No matter how big your problem, someone always has a problem that is bigger.

This is not meant to minimize your struggles. Often when you face adversity or are in crisis, your life loses a sense of purpose. Caring helps bring that sense of purpose back.

Look for ways to demonstrate caring that relate to your problems. Has a parent died? Join a support group with other kids who have lost parents and care about each other. Are you working to stop a bad habit? Dedicate time to helping other kids overcome addictions as well.

Think about your life and your current situation. What are some ways you can care for others?

A Story of Caring

Alex's Lemonade Stand is a charity that raises money for cancer research, but it wasn't started by just anyone. At age one, Alex Scott was diagnosed with a rare form of cancer. By the time she was four years old, she knew she wanted to give something back to the doctors who had helped treat her cancer and perform her surgeries. Alex asked her parents if she could sell lemonade to raise money to help other kids with cancer. That lemonade stand raised $2,000.

Alex and her family continued to hold the lemonade stand each year until Alex passed away. In the four years that they held the lemonade stand, Alex and her family raised over $1 million for cancer research. The little girl turned her fight with cancer into an opportunity to care about others, but the story doesn't stop there.

When Alex passed away, her parents needed a way to work through their grief. They started the Alex's Lemonade Stand Foundation. Since 2004, their foundation has raised over $50 million for cancer research. It has attracted the attention of celebrities such as singer Jordin Sparks and model Cindy Crawford. Lemonade stands have been set up throughout the United States to raise money for cancer research, and Alex's legacy lives on.

1. How do you think Alex's Lemonade Stand helped Alex and her parents through Alex's battle with cancer?

2. What do you personally think about what they did?

3. How does this story demonstrate the power of caring?

Equality

Take a look at these quotes about equality.

> "Don't be in a hurry to condemn because he doesn't do what you do or think as you think or as fast. There was a time when you didn't know what you know today."
>
> - Malcolm X

Does this quote remind you of any conflict or situations you have faced?

> The tears of the red, yellow, black, brown and white man are all the same.
>
> ~Martin H. Fischer

How can this quote help you as you're facing adversity or feeling like no one has ever gone through what you are going through?

> "I hate to complain...No one is without difficulties, whether in high or low life, and every person knows best where their own shoe pinches."
>
> - Abigail Adams

What does this quote from Abigail Adams say to you?

Often when you find yourself in a situation requiring resilience, you also find people who make you feel like an outcast, who are afraid to be around you or who ridicule you for the situation you're going through. Focusing on equality can help you develop resilience in two ways:

It reminds you that you are not alone in your struggles

To use equality as a reminder that you are not alone in your struggles, seek out other people who are facing similar challenges. If a support group does not exist for people who are going through similar struggles, create one. The goal of a support group is not to throw a large pity party for each other. It is to realize that you can use a spirit of equality and band together to build each other up and help each other get through your struggles together.

The Internet is a good place to look for others who are facing similar struggles. You do not have to meet with people face to face to support one another. Have a parent or teacher help you look for support groups to become a part of. They can also search for resources in your community that you may not know about or look for summer camps and retreats for people like you.

It gives you an opportunity to educate others

Maybe you have cancer or have been partially paralyzed and your friends are afraid to spend time with you. Maybe you are gay and feel isolated from your peers. By remembering that we are all equal and finding similarities between yourself and others, you can educate your peers.

This may involve reminding your friends that you're still the same person you were before being diagnosed with an illness or before being in an accident. It may involve starting a gay-straight alliance or another awareness group at your school to help students understand you better.

How can you use the idea of equality to help you through your struggles?

Summing It Up

1. What is resilience?

2. How can you develop resilience?

3. What situations in your own life could benefit from your increased resilience?

4. Now what? Now that you've learned about resilience, what are you going to do? How is your life going to change?

Resources to Learn About Resilience

Reading stories about kids who have developed resilience, even if they are fictional, can help you develop resilience in yourself. Get a parent or teacher to help you check out some of these resources that may help you with your specific situation.

Books About Death and Grief

When Dinosaurs Die: *A Guide to Understanding Death* by Laurie Krasny Brown

Everett Anderson's Goodbye by Lucille Clifton

Lifetimes by Bryan Mellonie

I'll Always Loves You by Hans Wilhelm

The Tenth Good Thing About Barney by Judith Viorst

Daddy's Climbing Tree by C.S. Adler

Books About Illness

Will I Still Have to Make My Bed in the Morning? by Barry Rudner

A Window of Time by Audrey O. Leighton

The Memory Box by Mary Bahr

Books About GLBT Issues

Daddy, Papa and Me by Leslea Newman

In Our Mothers' House by Patricia Polacco

We All Sing with the Same Voice by J. Phillip Miller

The Different Dragon by Jennifer Bryan

The Sissy Duckling by Harvey Fierstein

The Boy Who Cried Fabulous by Leslea Newman   E New

Uncle Bobby's Wedding by Sarah Brannen

Books About Abuse

The Boy Who Didn't Want to be Sad by Rob Goldblatt

Edwardo: The Horriblest Boy in the Whole Wide World by John Burningham

One of the Problems of Everett Anderson by Lucille Clifton

Sometimes My Mommy Gets Angry by Bebe Moore Campbell

A Family That Fights by Sharon Chesler Bernstein

A Safe Place by Maxine Trottier

Clover's Secret by Christine M. Winn

Don't Be Scared to Tell by Kathy Delgado Chatterton

Because It's My Body by Joanne Sherman

Books About Homelessness and Poverty

The Magic Beads by Susin Nielsen-Fernlund

A Chair for My Mother by Vera B. Williams

Fly Away Home by Eve Bunting

The Hard-Times Jar by Ethel Footman Smothers

Hope by Adam Eisenson

Books About Bullying/Harassment

Lucy and the Bully by Claire Alexander

Bootsie Barkner Bites by Barbara Bottner

King of the Playground by Phyllis Reynolds Naylor

The Ugly Duckling by Jerry Pinkney

Mr. Lincoln's Way by Patricia Polacco

Bullies Are a Pain in the Brain by Trevor Romain

Bully Trouble by Joanna Cole

The Bully Blockers Club by Teresa Bateman

Books About Other Life Challenges

Is a Worry Worrying You? by Ferida Wolff

There's a Big, Beautiful World Out There! by Nancy Carlson

On Those Runaway Days by Alison Feigh

Books About Immigration and Different Cultures

A Step from Heaven by An Na

Whoever You Are by Mem Fox

American Too by Eliza Bartone

The Dream Jar by Bonnie Pryor

Hannah is My Name by Belle Yang

I Hate English! by Ellen Levine

The Butterfly Seeds by Mary Watson

My Name is Yoon by Helen Recorvits

A Piece of Home by Sonia Levitin

Four Feet, Two Sandals by Karen Lynn Williams

GLOSSARY

Adversity – challenges or tough situations in life

Asset-Building – saving up money and other resources

Boundaries – limits

Character – a person's attitude and actions

Equality – treating everyone with fairness

Resilience – the ability to overcome challenges

Made in the USA
San Bernardino, CA
19 August 2014